FROM THE MOUNTAINS
TO THE SEA

OTTER POINT, ACADIA

MONROE BROOK, WHITE MOUNTAINS

FROM THE MOUNTAINS
TO THE SEA

Images from the White Mountains in New Hampshire
and Acadia National Park in Maine

PHOTOGRAPHS BY

CHUCK THEODORE

RIVENDELL ART PHOTOGRAPHY
FRANCONIA, NEW HAMPSHIRE

OTHER PUBLICATIONS BY CHUCK THEODORE
A White Mountain Calendar
A New England Calendar
A New England Engagement Calendar
Rivendell Art Cards
White Mountain Post Cards

FROM THE MOUNTAINS TO THE SEA
Copyright©1991 by Chuck Theodore
All rights reserved.
ISBN: 0-936647-23-X (Hardbound)

ISBN: 0-936647-24-8 (Softbound)

Library of Congress Catalog Card Number: 91-62062

First Printing, August, 1991

Design and layout by Chuck Theodore
Composition: The Lugie Press/DAK Designs, Manchester, New Hampshire
Printing and binding: Palace Press, San Francisco, California
Printed in Singapore
Rivendell Art Photography
Franconia, New Hampshire

To
My wife, Marcia
and
My son, Toby

BEGINNINGS

My first recollections of the White Mountains are as a child of 7 or 8. On a late September Sunday, Mom, Dad, my younger sister Jo-Ann and I piled into Dad's yellow Buick Century and headed north, away from Manchester. No interstate back then, just a journey up U.S. Route 3 through Concord, Laconia, Plymouth and to the mountains. We seldom traveled out of the city and when we did, it was either south to visit relatives in other cities or east to Hampton Beach where my grandparents owned cottages and where we would spend summer weekends and summer vacations. A trip to the North Country was a trip to another world, uncrowded, peaceful, very quiet.

Once we reached Lincoln, our route would be east over the Kancamagus Highway to what was then the sleepy mountain village of North Conway, north on U.S. Route 302 through Crawford Notch, then south through Franconia Notch. I still remember gazing in awe at mountains that seemed beyond reach, towering above me as we snaked our way through near wilderness. In the city, trees would change color, but here whole mountains did. It was exhilarating to see the reds, yellows, greens and orange in such joyful brilliance, a carpet of colors that touched the sky.

It was almost 15 years later before I returned, this time not to look at the peaks but to climb them. My dear friend now of 23 years, Chuck Flanders, and I set out to conquer Mount Lafayette. You would think that someone who had not done any serious hiking would have started out small and worked his way up. Nope. But hours later, as I stood 5,260 feet above sea level, with chest heaving, leg muscles throbbing and feet having been battered by every rock on the trail, I felt I was on top of my world. The pains slipped out of mind as I stared into the Pemigewasset Wilderness, south along the Franconia Ridge, and at mountain peaks and valleys everywhere, bathed in a soft, blue light. Voices faded into a distant background as a strong yet warm wind tugged at my hair, my shirt, pulling me into an experience of pure astonishment as I inhaled the beauty of Nature that surrounded me. The rewards were breathtaking.

I am still hiking these mountains.

———————

It was August of 1969, Woodstock had just ended and my fall semester at the University of New Hampshire was soon to begin. Vietnam, flower power, civil rights, rock music, ecology, feminism, social change, folk music, hawks, doves--the world was in turmoil with no signs of settling down.

An escape from this reality was offered by a friend, Mark Pitman. Camping. He told me of this place far up the coast of Maine where the mountains met the sea.

We left at midnight and soon were streaking up I-95 in Mark's bright orange BMW2002tii, windows open, wind blowing, slicing the darkness to the music of Jefferson Airplane, Jimi Hendrix, Janis Joplin, Buffalo Springfield, Spirit and others. We arrived in Ellsworth about 6 a.m., woke up Mark's girlfriend, had a beer or two, then drove the last leg of our journey and set up camp at Blackwoods Campground. Never will forget Mark's tent, a Sears model endorsed by Ted Williams. Almost as big as a cabin.

For the next 7 days, there was nothing wrong in the world. In fact, the world outside of Acadia seemed to cease to exist. Everyday was clear, sunny, in the low 70's, nights were star studded and near 50°. We hiked every day, doing Cadillac, Dorr, Gorham and Acadia Mountains and Champlain Mountain twice via Precipice, down to the Bowl, and over and down the Beehive. We walked the coast from Blackwoods to Sand Beach without setting foot on path or road. We watched the surf crashing at Great Head and seagulls gliding on wind currents, spiraling higher and higher. We saw sunrises that opened our eyes and sunsets that blew our minds. We listened to the campfire and found dreams in the flames. On midnight drives headlights would find deer, raccoons, rabbits, a fox, on our way to gaze at the stars from the summit of Cadillac Mountain or from a special place along Ocean Drive. I remember the first time I lay prone in the darkness, with a summer night's caressing breeze, spotting shooting stars and trying to comprehend the vast universe above and around, and my small part in it.

I have been going to Acadia for 22 years now, still listening, still searching for answers to questions I do not fully understand.

———————————

I did not know it at the time, but those days were the beginnings of this book. With this collection of images, my hope is to share some of the feelings and emotions I have experienced over the years in the White Mountains of New Hampshire and at Acadia National Park in Maine.

Chuck Theodore
August, 1991

FROM THE MOUNTAINS
TO THE SEA

MOUNT WASHINGTON, WHITE MOUNTAINS

SAND BEACH, ACADIA

FRANCONIA NOTCH, WHITE MOUNTAINS

GALE RIVER, WHITE MOUNTAINS

ARETHUSA FALLS, WHITE MOUNTAINS

SAND BEACH, ACADIA

MOUNTS LAFAYETTE & LINCOLN, WHITE MOUNTAINS

FRANCONIA RIDGE, WHITE MOUNTAINS

WINTER DREAMS, WHITE MOUNTAINS

FRESH SNOW, WHITE MOUNTAINS

WINTER WATCH 2, ACADIA

MOONRISE, WHITE MOUNTAINS

PAINTED WATER, WHITE MOUNTAINS

BIRCH BALLET, WHITE MOUNTAINS

UNTITLED, WHITE MOUNTAINS

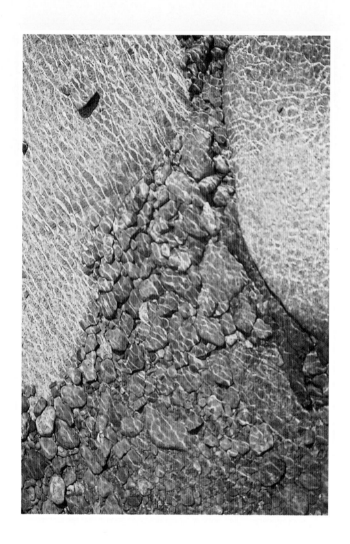

STREAMBED, WHITE MOUNTAINS

UNTITLED, WHITE MOUNTAINS

SUNSET, WHITE MOUNTAINS

LOVEMAKING, WHITE MOUNTAINS

SUMMER DREAMS, WHITE MOUNTAINS

SUNSET, EAGLE LAKE, ACADIA

UNTITLED, ACADIA

CHAMPLAIN MOUNTAIN, ACADIA

OTTER COVE, ACADIA

NORTHEAST HARBOR, MAINE

GREAT HEAD, ACADIA

SUNRISE, ACADIA

TREE STUMP, ACADIA

PURPLE HAZE, WHITE MOUNTAINS

PARRISH TWILIGHT, WHITE MOUNTAINS

LUPINE, ACADIA

PINK MOCCASIN FLOWERS (LADY SLIPPERS), ACADIA

ALPINE BLUETS, WHITE MOUNTAINS

OLD MAN OF THE MOUNTAINS, WHITE MOUNTAINS

SUNSET, ACADIA

SUNRISE, ACADIA

IN THE PEACE OF THE WOOD, WHITE MOUNTAINS

GALE RIVER, MOUNT LAFAYETTE, WHITE MOUNTAINS

LAKES OF THE CLOUDS, WHITE MOUNTAINS

PEMI OVERLOOK, WHITE MOUNTAINS

SUMMER DREAM, ACADIA

OTTER COVE, ACADIA

SUNSET, ACADIA

GREAT HEAD, ACADIA

OTTER POINT, ACADIA

GREAT HEAD, ACADIA

AFTER THE RAIN, ACADIA

OCEAN PATH, ACADIA

COFFIN POND, WHITE MOUNTAINS

FROM CHAMPLAIN MOUNTAIN, ACADIA

SUNSET, ACADIA

SUNSET, ACADIA

SURF, ACADIA

OTTER CLIFFS, ACADIA

PEMETIC MOUNTAIN, ACADIA

SUNSET, ACADIA

SUNSET, ACADIA

SUNSET, ACADIA

COFFIN POND, WHITE MOUNTAINS

OTTER POINT, ACADIA

LENTICULARS, WHITE MOUNTAINS

MONTICELLO LAWN, WHITE MOUNTAINS

SUNSET, ACADIA

TWILIGHT, ACADIA

THE BEEHIVE, ACADIA

JORDAN POND, THE BUBBLES, ACADIA

SUNSET, LAKE CHOCORUA, WHITE MOUNTAINS

SUNSET, SWIFT RIVER, WHITE MOUNTAINS

MOUNT LINCOLN, WHITE MOUNTAINS

FRANCONIA RIDGE, WHITE MOUNTAINS

STONE BRIDGE, ACADIA

PEABODY RIVER, WHITE MOUNTAINS

AUTUMN, ACADIA

SWIFT RIVER, WHITE MOUNTAINS

LAST SUMMER'S CONVERSATION, FRANCONIA, NEW HAMPSHIRE

SOMESVILLE, MAINE

PEMIGEWASSET WILDERNESS, WHITE MOUNTAINS

MOUNT LAFAYETTE, WHITE MOUNTAINS

HUNTINGTON RAVINE, WHITE MOUNTAINS

THE PRESIDENTIALS, WHITE MOUNTAINS

KANCAMAGUS HIGHWAY, WHITE MOUNTAINS

JORDAN POND, THE BUBBLES, ACADIA

GRAND VIEW ROAD, SUGAR HILL, NEW HAMPSHIRE

RED MAPLE, WHITE MOUNTAINS

BIRCH TREES, ACADIA

AUTUMN, WHITE MOUNTAINS

AUTUMN LEAVES, ACADIA

BIRCH & RED MAPLE, ACADIA

REFLECTIONS, SWIFT RIVER, WHITE MOUNTAINS

BEAVER POND, KINSMAN NOTCH, WHITE MOUNTAINS

GORHAM MOUNTAIN, ACADIA

LEAF & TWIG, WHITE MOUNTAINS

DEER, ACADIA

AUTUMN, ACADIA

AUTUMN LIGHT, ACADIA

BIRCHWOOD, WHITE MOUNTAINS

WINTER, ACADIA

CRAWFORD NOTCH, WHITE MOUNTAINS

MOUNT CHOCORUA, SWIFT RIVER, WHITE MOUNTAINS

MOUNT LAFAYETTE, WHITE MOUNTAINS

WINTER DREAMS, WHITE MOUNTAINS

ALPINE GLOW, WHITE MOUNTAINS

ABOUT THE PHOTOGRAPHS

The images in this book were made with Canon F-1, Canon A-1 and Canon Ftb cameras, and Canon lenses with focal lengths from 28mm to 400mm. Film used throughout was Agfachrome Professional, various speeds. The only filter used was a polarizer, the only light used was what was available. All compositions were full frame.

ORDERING PHOTOGRAPHS

Custom, hand-printed photographs of the images contained herein are available in sizes ranging from 7x10 to 30x40 inches. The photographs are signed and numbered and limited to 50 prints per image. The prints are coated to prevent fading and to protect against moisture and dirt.

For information on purchasing photographs and their availability, please write to Chuck Theodore, Rivendell Art Photography, Franconia, New Hampshire, 03580-0352.

Requests for information on other publications should be sent to the same address.

GALLERIES

In Sugar Hill, New Hampshire

Chuck Theodore's gallery in the White Mountains is open year round, seven days a week from late June through late October, and weekends the rest of the time. Hours are 1 to 5, Sunday, 11 to 5 Monday through Saturday. Directions: take I-93 to exit 38, Franconia, north on Route 18 a mile and a half, left onto Streeter Pond Road, less than a quater of a mile.

In Bar Harbor, Maine

A second gallery exists through the cooperation of the Acadia Corporation, a wonderful bunch of people. The gallery is located on the second floor of the Acadia Shop, 85 Main Street. It is open seven days a week, late May through late October.

A (VERY) BRIEF BIO

Chuck Theodore was born in New Hampshire, raised in New Hampshire and educated in New Hampshire. He attended the University of (you guessed it) New Hampshire from 1967 to 1972, nearly achieving a major in English Literature before diving headlong into Philosophy.

He's still in New Hampshire.

With no formal training, he began his career as a photographic artist in 1977. Since then he has sold thousands of photographs of his images to people throughout the United States and worldwide, and to libraries, companies, hotels, banks, etc.

Chuck moved to the White Mountains in 1980, where he now happily lives with his wife, Marcia, and their son, Toby. And five cats.

He vacations in Acadia.